Knock! Knock! Who's There?

ARCTURUS

This edition published in 2017 by Arcturus Publishing Limited
26/27 Bickels Yard, 151–153 Bermondsey Street,
London SE1 3HA

ISBN: 978-1-78428-615-6
CH005154NT
Supplier 29, Date 0517, Print run 5780

Written by Lisa Regan
Illustrated by Shutterstock
Designed by Trudi Webb
Edited by Tracey Kelly

Printed in China

CONTENTS

17

KNOCK, KNOCK.
WHO'S THERE?
MAUD.
MAUD WHO?
MAUD OF MONEY, THOSE MILLIONAIRES!

KNOCK, KNOCK.
WHO'S THERE?
HARRY.
HARRY WHO?
HARRY SPIDER IN THE BATH—WATCH OUT!

KNOCK, KNOCK.
WHO'S THERE?
TESSA.
TESSA WHO?
TESSA LONG TIME FOR YOU TO ANSWER WHEN I CALL!

25

29

35

39

45

52

70

71

KNOCK, KNOCK.
WHO'S THERE?
A TITCH.
A TITCH WHO?
BLESS YOU, DO YOU HAVE A COLD?

KNOCK, KNOCK.
WHO'S THERE?
MAVIS.
MAVIS WHO?
MAVIS BE A WARNING TO YOU!

KNOCK, KNOCK.
WHO'S THERE?
NANA.
NANA WHO?
NANA YOUR BUSINESS!

84

85

93

99

103

105

109

121

123

125

127

KNOCK, KNOCK.
WHO'S THERE?
HOUSE.
HOUSE WHO?
HOUSE ABOUT WE HAVE COFFEE AND CATCH UP ON THE GOSSIP?

KNOCK, KNOCK.
WHO'S THERE?
MORRIE.
MORRIE WHO?
MORRIE TRIES TO KISS ME, THE MORE I RUN AWAY!

KNOCK, KNOCK.
WHO'S THERE?
NORMA LEE.
NORMA LEE WHO?
NORMA LEE I'D RING, BUT THE DOORBELL'S BROKEN.

KNOCK, KNOCK.
WHO'S THERE?
ANDREW.
ANDREW WHO?
ANDREW ON THE WALL AND NOW SHE'S IN TROUBLE.

KNOCK, KNOCK.
WHO'S THERE?
RIOT.
RIOT WHO?
RIOT ON TIME THIS MORNING!

KNOCK, KNOCK.
WHO'S THERE?
OLLIE.
OLLIE WHO?
OLLIE WANT IS TO ASK IF YOU'RE PLAYING TODAY?

145

KNOCK, KNOCK.
WHO'S THERE?
LAUREN.
LAUREN WHO?
LAUREN ORDER IS VERY MUCH REQUIRED IN THIS TOWN.

KNOCK, KNOCK.
WHO'S THERE?
RUSSELL.
RUSSELL WHO?
RUSSELL ME UP A SANDWICH, I'M STARVING!

KNOCK, KNOCK.
WHO'S THERE?
RILEY.
RILEY WHO?
RILEY, RILEY NEED THE BATHROOM!

KNOCK, KNOCK.
WHO'S THERE?
TRIS.
TRIS WHO?
TRIS IS THE LAST STRAW—JUST LET ME IN!

KNOCK, KNOCK.
WHO'S THERE?
SIDNEY.
SIDNEY WHO?
SID NEEDS YOUR HELP TO FIX HIS CAR.

KNOCK, KNOCK.
WHO'S THERE?
ALF.
ALF WHO?
ALF-OLLOW YOU WHEREVER YOU GO!

157

158

168

KNOCK, KNOCK.
WHO'S THERE?
SHEILA.
SHEILA WHO?
SHEILA-PPRECIATE THOSE CHOCOLATES YOU BOUGHT HER.

KNOCK, KNOCK.
WHO'S THERE?
YVETTE.
YVETTE WHO?
YVETTE HAS BANDAGED MY POOR DOG'S TAIL.

KNOCK, KNOCK.
WHO'S THERE?
TEX.
TEX WHO?
TEX YOU AGES TO ANSWER YOUR DOOR!

175

KNOCK, KNOCK.
WHO'S THERE?
MARSHA.
MARSHA WHO?
MARSHA-MALLOWS IN MY HOT CHOCOLATE, PLEASE!

KNOCK, KNOCK.
WHO'S THERE?
RHODA.
RHODA WHO?
RHODA BIKE FOR THE FIRST TIME TODAY!

KNOCK, KNOCK.
WHO'S THERE?
NEIL.
NEIL WHO?
NEIL-LY FOOLED YOU, IT'S REALLY KEVIN!

185

195

KNOCK, KNOCK.
WHO'S THERE?
WANDA.
WANDA WHO?
WANDA WHAT YOU'RE DOING TODAY?

KNOCK, KNOCK.
WHO'S THERE?
OLIVE.
OLIVE WHO?
OLIVE YOU VERY MUCH!

KNOCK, KNOCK.
WHO'S THERE?
LISA.
LISA WHO?
LISA CAN DO IS SAY THANKS FOR ALL YOUR HELP!

213

221

228

KNOCK, KNOCK.
WHO'S THERE?
WATER.
WATER WHO?
WATER YOU DOING HERE?

KNOCK, KNOCK.
WHO'S THERE?
ALPACA.
ALPACA WHO?
ALPACA SUITCASE AND COME TO STAY FOR A WHILE!

KNOCK, KNOCK.
WHO'S THERE?
STAN.
STAN WHO?
STAN BACK, I'M KICKING THE DOOR IN!

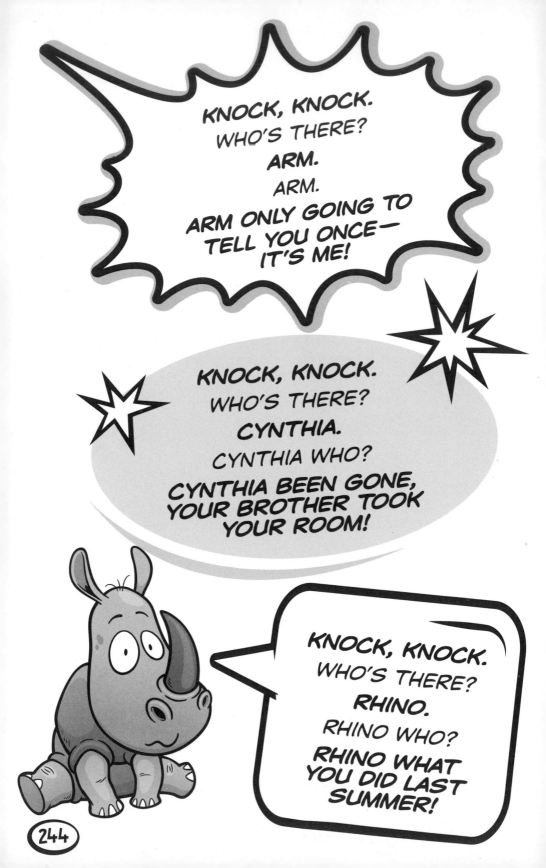